ECO-DISASTERS

DEADLY MINE

LIBBY, MONTANA

by **Kevin Blake**

Consultant: Bruce H. Alexander, PhD, Professor and Head
Division of Environmental Health Sciences
School of Public Health, University of Minnesota
Minneapolis, Minnesota

BEARPORT
PUBLISHING

New York, New York

Credits

Cover and Title Page, © Photo by Andrew Lichtenstein/Corbis via Getty Images; 4–5, © The University of Montana; 5, © NHAT V. MEYER/KRT/Newscom; 6–7, © Galyna Andrushko/Shutterstock; 7TR, © Diana Opryshko/Dreamstime; 7BR, © Turnervisual/iStock; 8, © Rick Bowmer/AP Photo; 9, © McGarvey, Heberling, Sullivan & /KRT/Newscom; 10T, © Onur ERSIN/Shutterstock; 10B, © ronstik/Shutterstock; 11L, © Chris Maddaloni/Roll Call Photos/Newscom; 11R, © JULIET EVANS/Alamy; 12, © asbestorama/iStock; 13L, USGS; 13R, © Alex Mit/Shutterstock; 14L, © Loren Callahan/AP Photo; 14R, © DmyTo/Shutterstock; 15, © Rick Bowmer/AP Photo; 16, © WoodysPhoto/Shutterstock; 17T, © Mikhail Storozhok-kasianenko/Dreamstime; 17B, © tammykayphoto/Shutterstock; 18, © Rick Bowmer/AP Photo; 19, © ANDREW SCHNEIDER/KRT/Newscom; 20, © WILLSIE/iStock; 21L, © Nutthika/Shutterstock; 21R, © MikeDotta/Shutterstock; 22, © AP Photo/Matthew Brown; 23, © Rick Sheremeta/AP Photo; 24L, © Rick Sheremeta/AP Photo; 25, © Ken Tannenbaum/Shutterstock; 26, U.S. EPA; 27T, © Congressional Quarterly/Newscom; 27B, © Susan Gallagher/AP Photo; 28, © Loren Callahan/AP Photo; 29T, © powerofforever/iStock; 29B, © shank_ali/iStock; 31, © Kim Britten/Shutterstock.

Publisher: Kenn Goin
Senior Editor: Joyce Tavolacci
Creative Director: Spencer Brinker
Photo Research: Editorial Directions, Inc.

Library of Congress Cataloging-in-Publication Data

Names: Blake, Kevin, 1978– author.
Title: Deadly mine : Libby, Montana / by Kevin Blake.
Description: New York, New York : Bearport Publishing, 2018. | Series:
  Eco-disasters | Includes bibliographical references and index.
Identifiers: LCCN 2017007495 (print) | LCCN 2017009476 (ebook) |
ISBN 9781684022229 (library bound) | ISBN 9781684022762 (ebook)
Subjects: LCSH: Asbestos mines and mining—Health
  aspects—Montana—Libby—History—Juvenile literature. |
  Vermiculite—Health aspects—Montana—Libby—History—Juvenile literature.
  | Asbestosis—Montana—Libby—History—Juvenile literature. | W.R. Grace &
  Co.—History—Juvenile literature. | Mineral industries—Corrupt
  practices—Montana—Libby—History—Juvenile literature. | Hazardous waste
  sites—Montana—Libby—History—Juvenile literature. | Libby
  (Mont.)—History—Juvenile literature. | Libby (Mont.)—Environmental
  conditions—Juvenile literature.
Classification: LCC RA1231.A8 B55 2018 (print) | LCC RA1231.A8 (ebook) | DDC
  615.9/25392240978681—dc23
LC record available at https://lccn.loc.gov/2017007495

For more information, write to Bearport Publishing Company, Inc., 45 West 21st Street, Suite 3B, New York, New York 10010. Printed in the United States of America.

10 9 8 7 6 5 4 3 2 1

Contents

Home Invader

As the golden sun set over Libby, Montana, in early 1963, Les Skramstad came home after a hard day's work at the local **mill** and **mine**. His wife kissed him at the door and his young kids playfully grabbed his legs. They didn't mind that he was covered in powdery brown dust. They were just excited to see him.

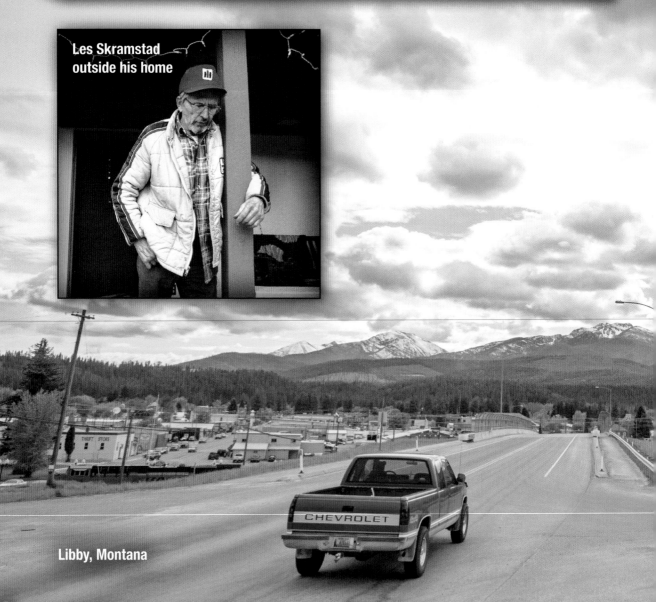

Les Skramstad outside his home

Libby, Montana

Little did Les know that the dust on his clothing and body was deadly. It wasn't just dangerous for Les or for the other people who worked with him at Libby's **vermiculite** mill and mine. It was a **hazard** for their families, too. Soon, many people in Libby would become extremely sick, including Les and his family. Eventually, the dust would poison nearly the entire town.

In the early 1960s, more than 130 of Libby's 2,600 residents worked at the vermiculite mill and mine.

ENTERING LIBBY

Underground Discovery

Libby, Montana, is nestled in a valley near the rushing Kootenai River and the jagged Rocky Mountains. **Prospectors** looking for silver, gold, and **lead** first settled in the area in the mid-1800s. They dug a string of mines, and, over time, a small picture-perfect town grew. Then an underground discovery changed everything.

Libby, Montana, is 72 miles (116 km) south of the Canadian border.

Early explorers called the area around Libby "the land of shining mountains."

In 1921, a local prospector named E.N. Alley was exploring a deep **mineshaft** near his ranch. He held a torch to light his way. Some shiny **ore** caught his eye, so he poked it with the torch. All of a sudden, E.N. heard a strange sizzling sound as the **mineral** heated up. Then, instead of burning, it started to pop like popcorn! Right before his eyes, the small bits of rock changed into puffy **accordion**-shaped pieces. E.N. had discovered the largest supply of vermiculite in the world!

Vermiculite is a shiny gray, yellow, or brown mineral. This is what it looks like before it's heated.

E.N. decided to give the lightweight, fire-resistant mineral he had found a special name. He called it Zonolite.

This is what vermiculite looks like after it's heated.

Staking a Claim

Most of the townspeople thought the fluffy mineral E.N. had discovered was worthless. However, E.N. dreamed about Zonolite's many uses. Because it was lightweight and fireproof, he thought it would make a great **insulator** for homes . . . and he was right. Soon after his discovery, E.N. started mining the vermiculite and built a mill to process it.

The vermiculite mine in Libby

By 1926, E.N.'s new mine produced more than 100 tons (91 metric tons) of vermiculite a day!

First, the ore was dug out of the ground. Then it was hauled to the nearby mill. There, the ore was crushed, causing huge **plumes** of dust to be released into the air. Then the crushed ore was fed through a series of screens to sort the rocks by size. Once sifted, the ore was sent to other plants to be heated. It was cooked at 2,000°F (1,093°C)—that's hot enough to melt gold or silver! As a result, the vermiculite expanded up to 15 times its original size. Finally, the pieces were bundled together and shipped throughout the country.

Plumes of dust

Miracle Mineral

Not long after its discovery, thousands of people across the United States were using Zonolite to insulate the attics and walls of their homes. Zonolite was used for other things, too. Because it **retains** water, it was mixed with garden soil. It was also used to make building materials, such as bricks and large blocks.

Grass growing in vermiculite

Eventually, Zonolite was used in as many as 15 million attics across the United States.

Marc Racicot, the former **governor** of Montana, remembers as a child putting "giant bags" of Zonolite "into the attic and walls of our home and emptying them into the garden." Zonolite became such a success that in 1963 a giant company called W. R. Grace bought the mine and the mill. Grace soon became the largest **employer** in and around Libby, hiring hundreds of workers.

Marc Racicot served as Montana's governor from 1993 to 2001.

The W. R. Grace building in New York City

GRACE

Hidden Danger

What residents didn't know was that more than just vermiculite was being mined in Libby. Most vermiculite is completely safe. However, the vermiculite in Libby was mixed with tiny pieces of a deadly mineral called asbestos. Whenever the mill processed the vermiculite, it released huge clouds of asbestos-filled dust into the air.

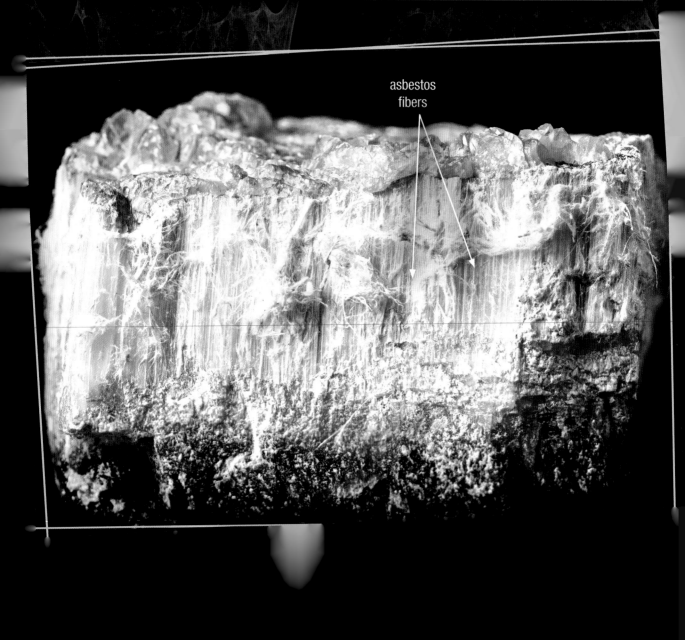

asbestos fibers

Asbestos is made up of **microscopic** strands, or fibers, that are 500 to 5,000 times thinner than a human hair. If a person breathes in these fibers, they can get stuck in the lungs. Over time, the fibers cause serious damage to healthy lung **tissue**. Breathing in a lot of the fibers can cause deadly **diseases**, such as lung cancer, mesothelioma, and asbestosis.

The type of asbestos in Libby's vermiculite is called tremolite. The fibers in tremolite are shaped like tiny needles. They can easily get stuck in a person's lungs, making them particularly deadly.

A microscopic view of tremolite asbestos fibers

Dust and More Dust

Asbestos-filled dust from the mill was everywhere in Libby. It was worst inside the mill where hundreds of people worked. The dust was so thick that workers couldn't see their hands on broomsticks as they swept up at the end of the day. Les remembered the dust from his first day at work. "Within fifteen minutes, I couldn't breathe. It was the worst I'd ever seen."

Each day, people like Les were forced to breathe in the dust while working at the mill.

Workers at the mill were given masks to help them breathe. However, the masks didn't **filter** out all the tiny, harmful particles.

It wasn't just workers who breathed in the dangerous dust. At its peak, the mill may have pumped 5,000 pounds (2,268 kg) of asbestos into Libby's air each day. On days when the wind was blowing toward the town, houses and shops would quickly become **shrouded** in a blanket of the deadly dust. People walking downtown would then breathe in the tiny asbestos fibers.

Some of the deadly dust would blow onto Main Street in Libby.

Asbestos Everywhere

Sadly, children in Libby were also **exposed** to the deadly asbestos. Kids would use their fingers to write their names in the dust that coated the sidewalks. The town also used vermiculite to cover the track near the high school. During races, runners who had fallen behind would have plumes of asbestos-filled dust kicked into their faces.

Students competing in a race

Libby also used vermiculite to line the Little League baseball field. "I had been exposed to it because it was put down on the baseball field where I played between the ages of eight and twelve," remembered Libby resident Dean Herreid.

Some kids in Libby played on huge mounds of Zonolite left around town. There were big piles of it, like mountains," recalls one Libby resident.

A child slides across a baseball field creating a cloud of dust.

Sick and Dying

With asbestos dust scattered all over town, the people of Libby soon became sick—very, very sick. Some residents came down with a terrible cough. Others experienced chest pain and difficulty breathing. "If you took a hot knife and stabbed me through the chest, that's what the pain feels like," said Dean Herreid. Gayla Benefield, another Libby resident, watched both her parents develop lung disease caused by asbestos.

yla Benefield's family was
kened by asbestos.

Gayla's dad, a miner, became so ill that he couldn't walk far without resting. Her mom suffered, too. "It took my mother seventeen months to slowly **suffocate**," Gayla remembers. "After that came the uncles and the aunts." Local nurse Kimberly Rouse saw many people in Libby suffer the same way. "It's the most **gruesome** death you can imagine." Now Gayla and her sister also have lung disease, along with three of their children. Gayla's grandchildren are now worrying about dying, too.

Les Skramstad and Gayla Benefield created a memorial to remember those who died from asbestos-related diseases.

As of 2016, at least 400 people have died from lung disease caused by Libby's asbestos. Nearly 3,000 residents are living with asbestos-related diseases.

No Help for the People

Shockingly, the W. R. Grace Company had known about the dangers of Libby's vermiculite dust for years. Yet they did little about it. In 1969, the company carried out a study of its workers. They found that 92 percent of employees who spent 20 years or more at the mill and mine developed lung disease.

W. R. Grace took X-rays of workers' chests and saw that many had damaged lungs. However, they never notified their employees.

Even with this knowledge, it took W. R. Grace decades to take even the simplest **precautions**. Eventually, they provided workers with special suits to shield their clothing from the dust. They also built showers for employees to use after a long, dusty workday. Introduced earlier, these safety measures might have saved lives, including Helen Budrock's husband, Art. "I think it would have helped," says Helen. "But he wasn't told the dust was dangerous. If he had known, he never would have worked there."

A shower at a factory

Mill and mine workers were told by Grace that the dust was nothing to worry about. The company said it was no more dangerous than dust from a field.

Special suits like this one can stop dangerous dust from getting on workers' clothes.

The Investigation

In 1999, a newspaper reporter from Washington state heard about a mining town in Montana where people were dying. He visited Libby and soon uncovered the awful truth. The reporter then wrote a series of stories, which got the attention of the U.S. government. Not long after, government scientists from the **EPA** (Environmental Protection Agency) flew out to Libby to investigate the jaw-dropping claims.

Workers check for asbestos.

In 2001, EPA scientists began **screening** people in Libby for lung disease. More than one-quarter of the townspeople had lung problems, including mesothelioma and lung cancer. The EPA also found dangerous levels of asbestos throughout Libby, including in homes and in the soil. Scientists called Libby "the worst case of industrial poisoning of a whole community in American history."

A sign warning people about asbestos in Libby

In 2002, the U.S. government declared the town of Libby a Superfund site. A Superfund site is a place that's polluted with hazardous materials and requires long-term cleanup.

Cleaning Up

The EPA soon started the difficult work of cleaning up the asbestos in Libby. Scientists visited more than 7,300 different locations, carefully removing dangerous asbestos from basements, attics, and other places. The hard work has helped. The amount of asbestos in Libby's air is 100,000 times lower than before the cleanup work began. However, there's still much more work to do.

Renting a Home or Apartment in Libby?

There is asbestos contamination in and around some Libby residences. Please ask the rental property owner about the results of the Environmental Protection Agency's inspection.

The EPA may be planning a cleanup at the property.

If you have questions about asbestos or cleanup, please call the EPA Information Center in Libby at 293-6194.

PA workers tested and removed sbestos from more than 2,000 cations around Libby.

Some of the forests around Libby are also contaminated with asbestos from decades of vermiculate mining. A Libby resident holds a handful of bark that may contain asbestos.

The asbestos cleanup is happening in more places than just Libby. That's because Zonolite was used throughout the country. The EPA has also investigated 200 other sites in Montana and across the nation to see if the product contaminated those places as well.

Zonolite was used in the walls of the World Trade Center in New York City. Some scientists worry that asbestos from Libby got into the air when the buildings collapsed on 9-11.

Some **estimates** show that there are up to 35 million buildings in the United States with Zonolite inside them.

Libby's Future

For many in Libby, the cleanup is happening far too late. Many have already died or become very sick. For others who appear to be healthy, they must wait and see whether they, too, will get sick. It can take up to 30 years or more for someone who was exposed to asbestos to develop health problems.

Libby, Montana

W. R. Grace closed the vermiculite mine in 1990. However, people exposed to the asbestos may get sick for years to come.

Libby is an ongoing **tragedy**. Not only did Les Skramstad get mesothelioma, but his wife and three of his four kids also got sick. "My grandpa lived to be 88, my dad was 78, I might be looking at 68," Les said two years before he passed away. Les died hoping that others would learn from the Libby disaster and help protect workers and their families. "I want justice. Justice for my family and my town."

Before he passed away at age 70, Les Skramstad tells government officials his story in hopes of preventing another tragedy like the one that struck the people of Libby.

Fixing the Future

Since the disaster in Libby, Montana, efforts have been made to help the victims and to clean up the town as well as to help prevent a similar catastrophe from happening in the future. Here are some examples.

More Cleanup

In 2008, W. R. Grace agreed to pay the EPA more than $250 million to help cover the cost of the huge cleanup in Libby. In total, nearly $600 million has been spent on cleanup efforts.

Speaking Out

Victims are speaking out to educate people about the dangers of asbestos. Norita Skramstad, Les's widow, said: "Our main goal is to stop it from going into the next generation. We have to see if it's still here. If it is, we've got to do something about it. All we can do is speak for those who have gone."

Norita Skramstad, Les's widow

Outlawing Asbestos

Under a law called the Toxic Substances Control Act, the EPA named asbestos one of the most dangerous **pollutants**. The law forced the government to take steps to reduce the amount of asbestos in the environment.

Money for Victims

The state of Montana agreed to give $68 million to more than 2,000 victims in Libby because it had failed to protect them from the asbestos danger.

Protecting Human Health

In 2009, for the first time in the history of the agency, the EPA declared a Public Health Emergency in Libby in order to provide federal health care assistance for victims of asbestos-related diseases.

Final Phase

The EPA is still cleaning up a few hundred properties in Libby and expects to complete the final phase of cleanup in two to three years.

Montana's capitol building in Helena

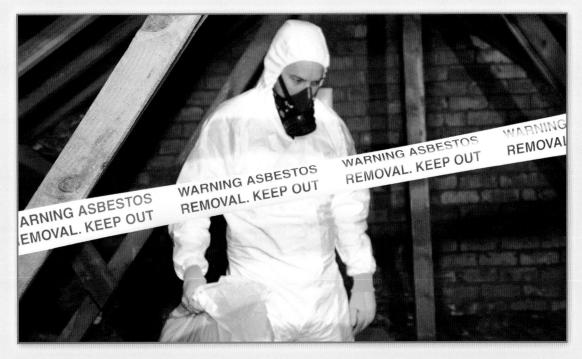

Asbestos removal requires special clothes and equipment to keep workers safe.

Glossary

accordion (uh-KAWR-dee-uhn) a long, portable musical instrument that has many folds

diseases (duh-ZEE-zez) illnesses

employer (em-PLOY-uhr) someone who hires and pays a worker to do a job

EPA (EE PEE AY) stands for "The Environmental Protection Agency"; a part of the government that enforces laws dealing with clean air and water

estimates (ES-tuh-meyts) to make careful guesses about the size, cost, or value of something

exposed (ik-SPOHZD) left open to attack

filter (FIL-tur) to remove unwanted material

governor (GUHV-er-nuhr) the head of a U.S. state

gruesome (GROO-suhm) causing horror

hazard (HAZ-erd) danger

insulator (IN-suh-lay-ter) something that does not allow the passage of heat

lead (LED) a soft, gray metal

microscopic (mye-kroh-SKOP-ik) able to be seen only with a microscope

mill (MIL) a factory that has machinery to process raw materials

mine (MINE) a deep hole or tunnel from which coal and other minerals are taken

mineral (MIN-ur-uhl) a substance found in nature; not a plant or an animal

mineshaft (MINE-shaft) a long tunnel that gives access to a mine

ore (OHR) solid material from which minerals or metals can be taken

plumes (PLOOMZ) long clouds of dust or smoke that rise into the air

pollutants (puh-LOOT-ants) harmful materials that damage the air, water, or land

precautions (pri-KAW-shuhns) steps taken to prevent an accident

prospectors (PROS-pek-turz) people who search for gold or other valuable resources

retains (ri-TEYNS) keeps

screening (SKREE-ning) testing people to see if they have a particular illness or condition

shrouded (SHROUD-uhd) covered

suffocate (SUHF-uh-kate) to stop breathing

tissue (TISH-yoo) a group of cells that forms an organ or other structure within a living thing

tragedy (traj-ih-dee) a horribly sad event

vermiculite (ver-MIK-yuh-lite) a soft mineral that expands when heated

Bibliography

Schneider, Andrew, and David McCumber. *An Air That Kills: How the Asbestos Poisoning of Libby, Montana, Uncovered a National Scandal.* New York: Penguin (2004).

Vollers, Maryanne. "Libby's Deadly Grace." Mother Jones (May/June 2000).

Walters, Joanna. "Welcome to Libby, Montana, the Town that Was Poisoned." The Guardian (March 7, 2009).

Read More

Bailer, Darice. *What's Great About Montana? (Our Great States).* Minneapolis, MN: Lerner (2014).

Goldish, Meish. *Poisoned Air: Bhopal India (Eco-Disasters).* New York: Bearport (2018).

Learn More Online

To learn more about the disaster in Libby, Montana, visit
www.bearportpublishing.com/EcoDisasters

Index

About the Author

Kevin Blake lives in Providence, Rhode Island, with his wife Melissa, son Sam, and daughter Ilana. He has written many nonfiction books for kids.